A Rhymer
REDEEMED

Karen Pierce

WESTBOW
PRESS®
A DIVISION OF THOMAS NELSON
& ZONDERVAN

Scripture quotations taken from the Holy Bible, New Living
Translation, copyright 1996, 2004. Used by permission of Tyndale
House Publishers, Inc., Wheaton, Illinois 60189. All rights reserved.

WestBow Press books may be ordered through booksellers or by contacting:

WestBow Press
A Division of Thomas Nelson & Zondervan
1663 Liberty Drive
Bloomington, IN 47403
www.westbowpress.com
1 (866) 928-1240

ISBN: 978-1-5127-4363-0 (sc)
ISBN: 978-1-5127-4364-7 (e)

Print information available on the last page.

WestBow Press rev. date: 06/03/2016

For my Great Grandpa, George Albigence Pierce
Who passed down his love of poetry
And especially for my family,
Who faithfully provide the rhyme and reason in my life.

Contents

Who Is He?

What Does He Do?

What Does He Want?

How He Loves Us!

Who Is He?

He is What He is

There was no cause that brought Him into existence
No event that foreshadowed His being
No power that unstopped his ears or opened His eyes
He has always been, all knowing, all seeing

He is an ungoverned God
Sadly for many, unknown
He is powerful, sovereign, but chooses to love us
Guiding us in Christ's Spirit, to become full grown

He is a faithful and unchanging God
Our shepherd, our way, our gate
Totally Holy and justified
Trust Him now to lovingly secure your eternal fate.

Everything Belongs to God

It all belongs to God!
How long I struggled with that in my heart
My pride and self importance
Refused to relinquish my part

My accomplishments and possessions
We're only partly due to Him
Some had come to me through my hard work
Some were just coveted and bought on a whim

How foolish was this perspective
His ownership not to recognize
The universe is His to rule
From largest mountain to things infinitesimal in size

And speaking of things of tiny size
My understanding was just as small
But now I happily acknowledge that
everything is a gift from God
And I had nothing to do with it at all

Limiting God

I have a friend who's afraid to be cremated
She thinks her old body will be needed
to create her glorified one
She forgets the original was created from a handful of dust
And for God creating is what He does,
from tree, to oceans, to stone.

A whale is no harder for Him than the tiniest ant
A whole universe He spoke into being
But we limit Him just as we limit ourselves
Forget He is almighty, all knowing, all seeing

We're more comfortable if He is no more powerful than us
No more creative than our tiny minds
We blindly stumble our way through our lives
Not looking too hard, afraid of what we might find.

We are currently the most supreme creatures on the planet
And we seem to think it's because we are so smart
God's word tells us it was part of His plan
And pride is something that should
have no place in our hearts

God demands that He be acknowledged
And if we're smart, we admit we are nothing alone
Surrender to Him, He will give you His strength
And with God living in you, there's no
limit as to what can be done.

Unwrap Your Gift

With a manger for a cradle
And oxen's breath to keep him warm,
It was a very simple beginning
For the greatest king that was ever born

His birth announcement was a star
And a choir of angels from heaven
Shepherds were the first to hear the news
Of the wonderful gift that the world had been given

Every Christmas, as long as time remains
We will be offered the gift once again
Will this be the year you unwrap yours?
And let your new life begin?

A Mother's Anguish

My baby, my son, my little boy
Caring for you was always an honor and a joy
I knew that you would never be completely mine
And that your purpose would take you from me in time

But as I stand at the foot of your cross
I realize that I scarcely understood the cost
How could this happen to my sweet boy
The Son of God so betrayed, his countenance destroyed

To see your beloved body so broken and bent
Made all the worse by the cruelty of evil intent
This pain I fear I cannot bear
I am numb and frozen with despair

How can I trust you, God, ever again?
When you allow my boy such horrible pain
And yet, my son, the Son of Man
Goes silently, willingly, to be part of your plan

To become the sacrifice, God's perfect lamb
So sin would be conquered, no longer a
wedge between God and man
I pray you take your son home and honor Him for eternity
Before he was your gift to the world, he
belonged for a precious moment to me.

Your God is Too Small

If your God resides on a cloud far away
And seldom moves from there at all
If his job of running the universe takes all his time
Then your God is way too small.

If he loves only a chosen few
And others not at all
If you understand his love as a human emotion
Then your God is way too small

If you believe in a God that has no plan,
And that the earth is a random spinning ball
That we climbed out of some primeval ooze
Then your God is way too small

My God created everything
And craves relationship with us all
His love is so great; He came to redeem us
For my God, it's no problem, He's big enough to do it all.

Child of God

Oh child of God, you are of the sky
With a soul that yearns to soar wide and high
Not knowing the Father,
Keeps you anchored earthbound
Where no authentic, true life
Can ever be found
Your spirit was created
To soar above solid land
It's only then, after trusting
You can finally see where you stand
Say goodbye to the world
With all its afflictions
And look to your God
To release all restrictions
Only He can take you
Where you need to be
To find purpose and joy
And be totally free.

Even Jesus Had A Few Bad Branches On His Family Tree

When Jesus was born in human form
He became as human as God can be
Tempted, tried, and rejected at times
And having no say over His family tree

His human lineage is full of failures
People trying but falling short
Serving as an example, yet today
Of what needing a Savior is all about.

Notorious folks you wouldn't brag on
Did your cousin throw his brother down a well?
Did your son commit murder for the sake of lust?
Or take his brothers birthright for no more than a meal?

The family tree hasn't improved much with age
A savior still being our greatest need
But we can be thankful that <u>our</u> lives aren't recorded
For thousands of years of posterity to read.

Jesus had some less than perfect human ancestors
And so have all of us yet today
But because of God's grace, our lineage includes a Savior
To change the outcome and show us the way.

Strange Goings On...

There's been some strange goings on
In Jerusalem this past week
Lots of us are scared and confused
We're just not sure what to think.

Most everyone is afraid of the rulers
And keeping their mouths shut tight
Even though they know in their hearts
That what's been done is just not right.

The Galilean whose name is Jesus
That's been healing folks miraculously
Has been arrested, beaten, scourged and mocked
And sent to die by hanging, nailed to a tree

The soldiers in charge of his execution
Decided his clothes they wouldn't tear
But cast lots to see which one of them
Would win his robe to wear

They hadn't seemed too worried
About the tearing of his flesh
The bruises and the battering
The crown of thorns placed on his head

He was hung between two thieves
The only innocent there
But asked forgiveness for his tormentors
And silently endured all the evil asked of him to bear.

This was the very same Jesus
Who just last week arrived triumphantly,
Hailed as King and lauded,
Now they've nailed him to a tree?

As he died, the earth trembled and shook
For hours the sky turned dark, an angry wind blew
I was afraid it was the end of the world
Pharisees ran from the temple as the
holy curtain split in two.

I heard they carried him to some rich man's tomb
And buried him inside
Then rolled a massive stone across the entrance
As though there was some shame they had to hide

When the women came early Sunday morning
To annoint his body in that tomb
They found the stone rolled away
And there was no one in that room

The burial clothes were neatly folded
But his body wasn't there
They say his friends then saw him alive!
Walking and talking, awake and aware.

His followers have spread miraculous tales
Of His appearing among them, to assure them he is alive
Some saw Him taken in a cloud up to heaven
He told of a coming baptism by fire and a
promise they too, would never die.

He always said his kingdom was not of this world
And claimed to be God's own son
The Messiah, foretold to come and save the world
Do you suppose He really was the one?

Only Two Things

There are only two things in the whole universe
God...and everything else
He exists outside of time and space
And will, long after our little world melts

God is not found in a tree, rock, or mountain
Although He created all of these
He is so much more than His amazing creation
We humans limit Him, our little minds to appease

The size of God we cannot comprehend
His love for us way beyond understanding
With power and might that are His alone
The heavens and earth heed His commanding

We mortals can't get over ourselves
We are so wonderously and intricately fit
Woven into all of God's creation
We like to think we had something to do with it

This arrogance will not go un-noted
God deserves the glory that is His just due
So we need to humble ourselves and let Him reign
And become all of what God wants us to

The Bridge

There was a chasm between man and God
So deep there was no end
God so Holy and man so sinful
There could be no relationship, no God as a friend

But God in his mercy, loved us so
He decided to build a bridge
And close the lonely separation
So love could flow from ridge to ridge

The bridge could not be made of mere wood
The sin would still be there
A perfect lamb must be the first to cross
And sacrifice for us, His very soul laid bare

He must take all the sin upon himself
Shed His blood, suffer and die
To cover the sin with righteousness
To make men Holy in God's eyes

The bridge was built, the lamb was sent
The sacrifice was made
So now God & man can know each other
No prayer unheard, misdirected or delayed

Some have never crossed the bridge
Though the way is clearly marked
The very same lamb who gave his life
Has shown us how to embark

How does one find this bridge?
It's built entirely of belief
And until a step is taken in faith
From sin there is no actual relief

Christ stands in the Chasm
And holds the bridge in place
To believe in his strength & sacrifice
Is what will let you cross and see God's face

The Gospel Goes Forth

The intent of God will not be changed
The word of God will not be hid
The apostles were jailed for preaching the truth
They refused to be quiet as man had bid.

But a jail won't hold salvations song
Nor the Belly of a whale
The bottom of a well is not deep enough
The word will go forth without fail

No desert wilderness, no sentence of stoning
No forbidding by men, no flogging,
no heavy burden to bear,
Will prevent the gospel from being told
The heart that God has touched, can't help but share

A Simple Man

Jesus, in general, was a very simple man
He taught in parables and other simple ways
His greatest conviction and criticism
Was saved for the so called, religious leaders of the day

He challenged their instructions to the people
And questioned their sincerity
He told them clearly, he could see into their hearts
And didn't care much for what it was He could see

The leaders began to fear Him
But mistook his peace for weakness
They grew bold in their plans to get rid of him
Not understanding it was God demanding
their submission and meekness

And because Jesus came from the Father
He longed to do His will
And tried his best to show the world the truth
Before He died on Golgotha Hill

So be sure you are ego free and have a clean, true heart
Remember all is visible to our Lord
Someday you'll fully understand his sacrifice and purpose
When you get to heaven and receive your eternal reward

Our Young Earth

Just how old is our earth?
The argument rages on
Scientists claim it's been here millions of years
Citing rock layers and fossils found in stone

The bible contains a different version
Says, we're not really all that old
It's all unfolded in 6 to10 thousand years
And creation took just 7 days, as God's account is told

But which-ever theory you believe
I don't find it necessary to take a side
I only know two things for sure
God is the one who put it all here,
And as for the end of it....He alone will decide.

The Legacy of Christ

I, Jesus, having been given authority
by God over all things
From the largest of mountains to
the hummingbirds wings,
Have left the earth, my work here being done
But, for those who believe, your work has only begun.

The world left me with no possessions to give
But I'm leaving you with all you need to fully live
My peace and joy I have passed to you
And my spirit to guide you into all that is true

I have given you my words, wisdom, teachings and love
I have granted you access to God the Father above
Now I give you a charge and a responsibility
To further the Kingdom, to tell others about me

To show the world what can be found in the light
Their spirits with God and the Son to unite
And when this unity is perfected into one
Then your work and mine will finally be done

The Next Christmas Morning

The very first Christmas was silent
It was nighttime and desert cold
The greatest gift that was ever given
Came in peace and calm as was foretold

But another Christmas is coming
As the gift returns to earth
To claim His people and rescue His church
It will be quite a change from His humble birth

He will appear in the fullness of His glory
Through the clouds of heaven, all will see Him come
Clothed in majesty and splendor
There will be no doubt where He comes from

Trumpets will sound and the heavens will ring
I imagine a rather noisy affair
But He is coming to take us home
So no matter how loud it is, I hope that you'll be there.

Wonderfully Made

As you awake and begin each and every day
I so hope you're aware that you <u>are</u> wonderfully made
From two tiny cells, each smaller than a grain of sand
You were formed in love by the Father's hand.

Those three miniscule bones in your inner ear
Placed there so the word of God you could hear
Your newborn soft and malleable bone
It strengthens & lengthens, 10 times
over before you are grown

Your brain that stores the memories
of every sight you have seen
Your soul that contains the essence of
what makes you a unique being
The complex digestive system that nourishes you
And builds and repairs your cells at the same time too

Your heartbeat that provides the rhythm of your days
The muscles and tendons that interweave with the clay
Your blood, your skin, your immune system, your eyes
All the wondrous, intricate workings unseen, inside

And when God was finished with this miracle called you
He loved you so much that He wasn't quite through
And in the fullness of God's own creativity
He placed a bit of it in all of us, including you and me

It's beyond our understanding, the miracles that we are
That we were designed in the image
of the creator of the stars
And, whether you sing or dance or paint, or write poetry
God is always glorified when you share His gifts, joyfully

Psalm 139:14
"I praise you because I am fearfully and
wonderfully made; your works are wonderful
I know that full well"

Who's Your Daddy?

Earthly parents are necessary
Even our Lord had some
But Jesus knew who He belonged to
And where it was that He came from

If you've had parents that have let you down
And your life so far is not what it could be,
Your Heavenly Father knows who you are
And has plans to prosper you and set you free.

If you've had an earthly daddy
Who was into raging and drinking?
And your earthly mama wasn't strong
And did the crying or the leaving

There is a savior named Jesus
Who does the forgiving and the saving
Your Heavenly Father loves you
Without wavering or changing

If your life so far has been a mess
It does not need to remain that way another day
There's an amazing life waiting for you
With a loving heavenly Father to show you the way.

Lord And Savior

Is Jesus Christ your Lord <u>and</u> Savior?
Or did you just ask Him for the Savior part?
Making Him Lord of your life is a little harder
It means offering completely, your mind & your heart.

As soon as we realize how powerless we are
We beg for help, provision and intervention
The following and serving Him requires a bit more
But it completes our surrender and reflects our intention

The day I first heard and trusted the good news
I believed,but couldn't give up my, self regard
I rejoiced in all God's promises of help
Still, wasn't so willing to work in the vineyard

It's like out of my need, I created Him
Instead of the other way around
My weakness provides reasons for wanting His help
But His expectations and rewards
are much more profound

You've been offered a savior without even asking
Now make Him also your Lord
Return His love and work for His kingdom
Living with Jesus, our Lord & Savior,
will be your eternal reward.

What Does He Do?

A New Day Dawning

It doesn't matter how long or how dark the night
It doesn't matter the depth of the chasm yawning
Every morning there's a chance to start again
Every morning a new day dawning

How faithful our creator, to promise us a new start
And no matter on which day you've begun
He is waiting always with open arms
To make you as new as the rising sun

And just as the sun emerges from darkness
Crests the mountain and crosses the sky
Your life can become a victorious thing
In Him, your joy can climb as high

Listen carefully for your God
His loving voice is always calling
Then rest awhile in His wonderful peace
And thank Him each morning for a new day dawning

Always Watching

You know that God is always watching you
Do you sometimes hope for a cloudy day?
Thinking that thousands of miles of atmosphere
Will obscure his view & He will not see you stray?

Silly child, playing games with yourself
Holding tight onto your pride
Anything but to admit your smallness
Next to the power and might on Heaven's side

Know now that He watches out of love
And see what happens to your fear
Trust His plan and His sovereignty
Look up and seek Him, He is always there.

Guilty

You say that guilt still consumes your life,
Are you sure it's God that's convicted you?
You have prayed for forgiveness and turned from your sin
You just don't know what else you can do.

The evil one loves to keep you in the past
Frozen there in your shame
He knows he can keep you from change or growth
By shutting you down with useless guilt and self blame

If you've sincerely asked, then you have been forgiven
Spend no more time considering your past sin
Seek the fellowship of God and remember His promises
He is the God of redemption, this
battle He will help you win!

Praying in the Spirit

The question was posed this morning,
What exactly does "praying in the spirit" mean?
Then Pastor Eric led us through the steps
Until the answer was clearly seen.

To give your mind to God,
To offer Him your body too,
Then let Him have control of the spirit
And let that spirit pray for you.

It means not letting any worldly need or want
Creep into your prayer
Your only goal, to be deep in the spirit
And have God meet you there

Then the Spirit will commune
With both the Father and the Son
They will all together pray over you
Without you uttering a single word one

This is what I think praying in the spirit means,
It requires total surrender of body & spirit & mind
Trusting your every need will be met
Just one kind of prayer, but perhaps the best kind.

Involved

Can you believe there are still some people?
Who believe that Jesus is *not* involved in their lives?
Who do they think comes to their rescue?
When the seas are rough and the boat about to capsize?

I mean, how much more involved could He get?
Giving up Heaven for men?
Giving it all to teach and to heal
To suffer and die and take on our sin?

To love us beyond understanding
To count every hair on our heads
To intercede with God himself
To stand against deserved wrath and
judgement in our steads.

Maybe the debt is too big to think about
So we deny it and go our own way
But, Jesus is very involved in your life
From your birth to your very last day.

Joy

The gift of joy feels like a strange concoction
And impossible to describe what
the heart is going through
Part excitement, part enthusiasm & part exhilaration
All inadequate descriptions, but the
best we seem able to do.

Other emotions command some sort of response
Like tears or flight or a tender embrace
Joy, is the only one that demands nothing from us
It frees us completely to be everything
needed in that time & space

We don't worry about who is watching
Joy is observable but cannot be directly shared
It's kind of a wonderful, inside sort of feeling
That causes the soul to be confidently bared

Those who see joy always want some for themselves
But no one has the recipe for sharing
It comes to us as a gift from the Holy Spirit
As we unwrap his love and caring

The best way we can share this pure love
Is to reveal Jesus, Our savior and God's son
And when people come to believe and trust
The spirit bestows joy, of their very own

Baptism Day

There's excitement and love surrounding you today
From your brothers and sisters on earth
Your decision to obedience in Christ our lord
Has led you to this new birth.

However this little party of ours
Is nothing compared to what heaven has unbound
There is rejoicing and singing and celebration
Over one who was lost and now is found

The angels are dancing there's music and joy
And all of it is just for you
Come up from the water washed white as snow
You are a changed creation, all brand new

So rejoice with all of us on your baptism day
The Holy Spirit has come to live in you
The special joy announcing your new life,
Is a gift God keeps on giving your whole life through.

Retreat Treatment

Thank you Father, for bringing us
To your healing mountain top
Teaching us with your tender love
To break down our walls and stumbling blocks

To be held in the arms of your daughters
Each one with a story of her own
Seeking all it is you have for us
Sharing strength and encouragement, we were never alone

Teach us to be grateful for discipline
Your careful pruning that helps us grow
Let our fruit be enough to share with the world
So your precious Son, they will come to know

Thank you for abiding with us
From mountain top to valley floor
Bring us to glory and righteousness
Give us wings and free our spirits to soar

Side Blessings

I was up early, enjoying my morning
When "Writer's Group" popped into my head
How it started out about getting writers together
But how God has used it for a hundred
"side blessings" instead

It's not really about our writing,
But it's about the people God has sent
And how He is using us to bless each other and Himself
By providing a place in which to love and to vent

God knows why He sent each one there,
And how difficult it was to overcome
The doubts, the shyness, the fear of judgment,
What each one was longing for and
where each was coming from

Who needed a touch, acceptance or a hug,
To make their joy increase and multiply
What kinds of things, using our little group
He could ease or erase or originate or magnify

All of these are "side blessings"
And teaches me God wastes not one single thing,
That He can use to accomplish His plan
Even a little group who started out, just writing.

The Bodyguard

Are you being tormented, and feel betrayed
By so called friends, you thought you knew
Did you ever think to call on the
biggest, baddest, bodyguard
That you have always had access to.

Your heavenly father will not avenge you
But will give you calm and peace
A confidence that no one can really hurt you
When you keep Him in your innermost place

Because He loves you, He will protect you
Keeping you unto Him alone
Stay patient, kind and loving
Perfect relationships will come along

The Caregivers

God's will and purpose have put you here
To care for some that He holds dear
Their bodies and minds now far from sound
But still He chooses to keep them around

It's so hard to be the loving refuge
Your only one person and their needs are huge
Just remember, you don't have to do this alone
God's love is sufficient til He takes them home

Old Owies

Do you have an old, ancient owie?
That you covered with a band-aid long ago
You know the wound is still festering under there
There are many clues that tell you it's so

You think about it day and night
There is still some actual pain
You see constant reminders of the damage it caused
All of these still remain.

You have asked God for healing
You have turned your life another way
And yet the ugly thing is still there
You're afraid it's here forever to stay

Are you sure you should trust your senses?
Over what God has promised you?
The "owie" has been forgiven
And it's only your mind that keeps it in view

So bravely rip that band-aid off
And view your healed skin
That owie was actually healed the minute you asked
Be amazed by His love again.

The Big Picture

When we someday see the big picture
In the sweet bye and bye
We'll have all the answers to all the questions
We will finally know why

Why that thing we wanted so bad
Was kept from us for years
Why that child died or that friend failed
Does God really count every one of our tears?

We seldom spend time discerning God's plan
And yet have plenty of plans of our own
What lessons did we fail to learn?
Just how high, could we have flown?

The answers will all be there
We'll know the goal was always for our good
Wrapped up in God's amazing love
That we so long misunderstood.

A Promised Land

God gave his people a homeland
As promised, it was theirs for the taking
But it took more than "come in, make yourself at home,"
The struggle was years in the making.

There were giants to conquer, walls to tear down
And souls to encourage to try
There were claims to be made on the promises of God
Lots of hard work and some tears to be cried

But along with the land God stood by his people
He gave them cities established, for living in
He gave them vineyards and olive groves
they did not have to plant
Asking only to be first in their hearts
and that they turn from their sin.

If all of this sounds a little familiar
And yet you've never crossed a river
or built an altar of stone
The journey from darkness to truth and light
Feels kind of like the Israelites coming home.

The Faith of a Mustard Seed

Whose ego does not quicken
At the reading of these familiar lines
All you need is the faith of a mustard seed
And the place of a mighty mountain you can realign

Do you recognize your desire to be powerful?
Known as a famous mountain mover
Would you set to work solving all your problems?
Daily easing your life as a miracle doer?

No more asking and waiting for God
I could move that mountain into the sea
There a just a few things wrong with this scenario
And the tiny mustard seed holds the key

The mustard seed is tiny
But never questions its fate,
It will grow to be a mighty tree
But on God it patiently waits

And when it has grown into that mighty tree
Its only purpose and design is to serve God's need
Its faith rests in the fulfillment of God's great plan
And the willingness to grow into more than a seed

So it's true that if your faith equaled
that of the mustard seed
God could use you to accomplish wondrous things
But your heart, mind and purpose must be to serve God
Or that mountain ain't moving, unless God gives it wings.

Upper Management

Looking for the perfect job?
With the perfect boss, location and perks?
God has a position chosen especially for you
Without lunchroom politics and co-worker quirks

You won't have to go in to interview,
He already knows your qualifications
The job is life-long, you'll never be laid off
And so full of joy, you won't need vacations

He will even send you a personal assistant
To supply daily knowledge and wisdom
The growth is steady, the work is rewarding,
And the retirement is out of this world & then some

This job is available to whoever will claim it
It's offered to many everyday
Unfortunately many will also turn it down
Thinking it's too hard or too much out of their way

I hope you will consider
Employing yourself in the "serving God" game
And sign up today for the job of a lifetime
Believe me, your career will never be the same!

Want to See What My God Can Do?

Want to see what my God can do?
There are miracles happening all around you
Some are everyday miracles, like life in the womb
Some even greater like life from a tomb

He can turn a pet scan from black to white
And heal a broken heart that has ceased to fight
Sending his people to the greatest need
Opening prison cells when He needs people freed

His church is a miracle in and of itself
It has flourished for centuries without
encouragement or wealth
It continues to grow despite persecution and oppression
With the love of Christ & the joy of
salvation being it's outward expression

Look into the heart of a friend
Feel the strength of the promise on which we depend
Expect a miracle with each rising of the sun
My God will accomplish all that needs to be done

When Courage Fails

Often courage and faith fail us
Right at the edge of a broken heart
The pain overwhelms our strength
The fear causes peace to depart.

We pray for strength greater than our pain
And belief stronger than our fear
A small remnant of hope and peace
A bit of comfort to dry our tears

These prayers aren't always answered
At least not so we can tell
And it's only later when we look back and see
God had His arms around us, keeping
us, as always, safe and well.

Where Am I Going?

Many people spend half their lives
Searching for this answer
It doesn't matter if you're grown & have already pursued
A life as a truck driver, teacher, or ballet dancer.

Why am I here?
What does life mean ?
How should I live?
Are things really as they seem?

Everyone asks these questions,
Some from a very young age
We think we can actually figure this out
Get the perfect answer and turn a new page.

Of course the problem & the folly come about
From looking within our own mind
We are never going to be smart enough
We are small & mortal & basically blind

But God has a purpose for each of us
A part in His grand plan,
So looking up & out, instead of down and in
Can make you a purposeful, accomplished,
living with meaning, kind of man.

Day of Salvation

Some people know the exact moment they were saved
And changed in the twinkling of an eye
But my journey has been full of fits and starts
And my wandering off the path, life
many times going awry

I don't understand why this is
And in the end, I believe, it doesn't matter
Though I envy some their dramatic experience
God chose for me, one rung at a time, up the ladder.

As long as we end up with the Lord
Does it matter if it comes in years or a snap
We do have to fully accept what He's offering us
And maybe I was always, just barely, holding back .

I spent a full ten years away from the Lord
I think they call it back-sliding
I was one of those where the seed fell on a rocky path
And with no roots and no encouragement,
there was no abiding.

Protected by no armor, I went the way the enemy led
Down the path of trusting the world and man
Satan is glib and charming and knows exactly
What it is we like to hear from him.

My childhood loneliness, my sense of self worth
And an intimacy I never had
An unwanted divorce, responsible for 4 kids and a dog
I moved into a new life of sad.

There followed years of selfish and shame
I was wallowing in evil attacks
Then finally, broken, I knelt by my bed
And begged Him to take me back

I gave up most of my excuses
My need for revenge and my pride
And He has never once since mentioned my past
My bruises and shame, I no longer need to hide.

The past really is the past
I've been forgiven, joy is complete
All but the lessons, left at the cross
There is no condemnation at the mercy seat.

In the Moment

Being "in the moment" is a lot harder than it looks
There are gazillions of distractions, vying for your mind
It takes so much practice, I had to break it down
And do a week, one day at a time.

Monday: The day I chose to be in the moment
Staying aware of my physical being
And so while walking and throughout the day
I concentrated on what my body was doing

The roll and rotation of all my joints
My muscles, fingers and toes
The beat of my heart, the filling of my lungs
The wonder and intricate nature of all of those.

Tuesday: I moved my attention to the world outside
Everything that I saw or that touched me
The dirt under my feet, the wind on my skin
The beauty of the world that surrounds me

Wednesday: The people around me were my focus
Those close and those I didn't know
Were they messengers or lessons or just to be loved
Vowing not to simply pass them by,
I tried to see them as a soul.

Thursday: Love and joy, and all things unseen
Were my Thursday's concentration
The supernatural love of God, prayer & the Holy Spirit
The power that holds the world
together, the colors of emotion

Friday: I decided that Friday would be Blessing day
How much had I been given?
All the ways God looks after me
Proving His love and care with each minute decision

The people He brings into my life
The guidance, sometimes unseen, He gives
The gift of Salvation and eternal communion
The reassurance in my heart, that He lives

Saturday: Time to take myself out of the picture
And think for the day about *His* plan
His power & sovereignty, control of the nations,
About the saving of His greatest creation, fallen man

Sunday: What does it feel like to really, fully rest
To destroy every ounce of worldly lust
To empty oneself of all but God
To learn to be still with total trust.?

This exercise was good for me
To practice in the moment living
But I need to repeat steps one through seven
Every week, for as long as I live, to reassure my awakening.

Money

I had no money and I was afraid
What if I ended up on the street?
I know that fear is not from God
And my needs He promised He would meet

But still, I worried and finally I prayed
Dear Lord, keep me encouraged & following you
He said, "What is it that upsets you child?"
I answered, "I'm unable to do all I want to do"

He then showed me how much I have
The stuffed closets, the pantry overflowing
The car in the driveway, a healthy family
My salvation and forgiveness, His word for my knowing

Rest quietly in my arms, He said,
Then turn and follow me
Your life is not in the things you have
But in Christ Jesus, where I designed for you to be

When I stop and think about it
My real needs are actually very few
And God will provide for me abundantly
Giving me real wealth, all that He has promised you.

Someday Soon

The world wants you "progressive"
And provides lies for you to listen to
The words that seep into your brain
Until you're numb to the evil thing
Someday soon, God will deal with you

The stuff our culture now allows
Should give the Lord a heart attack
Is there no shame? Is nothing too much?
Where is human dignity, respect and such?
Someday soon, as promised, He will act

The evil that walks unfettered
All across our land
Is winning the war
As never before
Someday soon, it will be taken in hand

Don't let the junk overwhelm you
Or lull you off to sleep
Make no mistake
Between real and fake
Someday soon, His promise He will keep

It makes me sad to see so many
Always choose the wrong way
I'm not sure if they're just lazy,
Their learning incomplete or their thinking hazy
Someday soon, the chance for change will be taken away

When God's plan and purposes are complete,
Then this world will come to an end
Evil will be locked away
People no longer, held in its sway
And I will be with my Lord in heaven.

Will I see you there?

Who's Got Your Back

Just who does this Satan think he is
Getting all up here in our face
I don't know about you, but I'm calling on the Lord
And putting this dude in his place

Satan already knows that the One in us
Is stronger than he that's in the world
But he counts on the fact that he can distract us
With fear and dread, when troubles swirl.

Hold on tight to Jesus' hand
Keep your heartstrings attuned to His
Trust that He will guide you through
He loves you, he's got your six

What Does He Want?

Are You Available?

Looking for fame and fortune?
Accolades from your fellow man?
They will never compare
To the glory you'll share
When you are used to accomplish God's plan

God needs you humble and available
No special skills are required
Just follow His lead
He will show you the need
And provide the strength when you are tired.

God's Will

Oh how we struggle and beg and plead
For signs from heaven, God's will to heed
The not being able to discern what to do,
Leaves us frozen and waiting, being pulled in two

Would your heavenly father cause you that strife
To leave you figuring out what He wants for your life
Certainly not, He will tell you in no uncertain terms
(You do need to ask Him, then listen
and be willing to learn.)

Moving to Shechem

Don't move to Shechem or anywhere else
Without God leading you
Even if you are perfectly, humanly able
Outside His will, it's the wrong thing to do

Look for the pillars of the guiding God
They should be in front of your eyes
If you can't see them because they're behind you
You'll put Him back in the lead if you're wise.

Smarter Than A Bunny

My dog brought me a bunny, he found in a bush
Frightened and nearly dead
The kids made him a comfy bed in a box
With love they patted his head

But that little rabbit never surrendered
To the help we were trying to give
And in his frantic need for escape
Gave up his chance to live

Lord, let us be smarter than bunnies
And learn the lesson well
That when we feel trapped and afraid
You came to save us, our fears to quell

Let us trust in your love and caring
And be comforted by your presence
To have no fear in total surrender
To know that love is your very essence

The "Real" Color of Man

For all of man's intelligence
And his creative, problem solving mind
He may be the dumbest animal around
Always at war with his own kind.

Most created beings do not question their color
Maybe they know it's provided for their protection
Man, however, uses color to categorize
Or as a reason for pride or hate or rejection

What if all humans were yellow or green?
Spotted, striped, blue or burnt umber
How would they judge friend from foe?
Or discriminate against each other?

After the war is over, the evidence will appear
Every man's bones are white, every man's blood is red
But God in His wisdom, gave our souls no color
They are filled with the creators love instead.

Present Time

When you opened your eyes this morning
You assumed you'd awakened in present time,
But was your heart or mind or soul
Lost in the past, contemplating some long ago crime?

Satan loves to keep you partially present
Where your whole heart cannot be given to the Lord
Whether it's anxiety or shame or just the world
He knows how to keep you upset or
worried, excited or bored.

Pray for forgiveness and cleansing
Then believe it has been done
Bring all of you as a gift to God
Claim the victory as already won

Banish Satan to the past
Along with all the other old ways
And wake up tomorrow fully present
For this and all the rest of your days.

Be Still

Surrender is a word you have seldom used
You were born with a will of steel
And it will take the refiner's mighty fire
To change the way you think and feel

Being still is *not* just sitting quietly
But it is a ceasing to strive
A surrender of our willful selves
And letting God decide how we will thrive

Until we are able to master this
We will eventually fail in all we do
We must trust, let it all go and let God,
Lead us where He would have us go

Psalm 46:10 Be still and know that I am God

My War

The war is raging every day,
Every minute, every hour of life I face
My sinful nature wants what it wants
At war with the Holy Spirit, who is
well armed with love & grace.

Every time I choose which side I'm on
I strengthen one combatant or the other
There is no claiming Swiss like neutrality
I'm in the fight of my life, and it's well worth the bother

I can defend myself, with the armor of God
Flex my spiritual muscles with help from within
Stay on the path that leads to life
And allow the spirit to make me more like Him

Forgiveness

There is more than one facet to forgiveness
More than a simple emotion to recognize
My forgiveness is no more difficult than yours to bestow
The severity of the crime is best evaluated in God's eyes

I've prayed for strength to forgive lots of times
And yet my heart remained unchanged
Could I blame it all on a fallen world?
So far from me, the murderers and the deranged

I was trying to feel emotional love for them
The enemies that stole my family's lives
The one that molested my children & disillusioned my life
The ones I most despised.

Was my non-forgiveness based in arrogance?
After all, I am better than they
The rules I have broken not as bad as theirs
I doubt those others even felt a need to pray

Or does God see my sin as equal to theirs?
That is hard for me to accept
Even though I haven't ever taken a life
To God, what does my unforgiving heart reflect?

If I can forgive and release them to God
Will my family feel betrayed?
Like I have switched sides and no longer support them
And hate me that their perpetrators I forgave?

That's when I recognized that old arrogance again
I can't undo another's sin and only God can forgive
But I can let go of revenge and bitterness
Let God do the judging and only worry
about how He wants me to live.

Gossip

Whispered words flying
Passed with a nod and a wink
With a sense of self importance
Never stopping to think…

The person being talked about
Has no chance to defend or reply
It's being attacked by an unseen enemy
The stain spread unjustly, usually a lie

The gossiper never realizes
The damage that may have been done
The accusations sent anomalously
The gossiper seemingly safe from harm?

What if gossip always returned?
Sent back like a wrongly addressed letter
Then the tables would be turned
And would reveal the initiator.

There is a reason we're told not to bear false witness
For the acid produced will surely erode
The vessel that it's carried in
Faster than the one on whom it's poured

If You Need Me Today, Lord

If you need to speak to me today, Lord
I'm afraid you may have to shout
My feelings are numb, my thoughts are scattered
From here to there and all about

I know your Holy Spirit is near
But you feel so far away
If you need to guide me today Lord,
You'll have to stand in my way

I'm not sure why my thoughts are far from you
But alone, I struggle to get them reversed
And I sit and worry, concerned with myself
When there are blessings to others to be dispersed

If you need to change me today Lord
And have some work for me to do
I'm counting on your strength and grace
To help me listen and trust and follow you.

The Hands and Feet of Jesus

God is sovereign and powerful
Unfettered by time or space
But some of His very best work has been done
By humble members of the human race

Those who carry the Holy Spirit
Become Jesus' hands and feet
And some who have been blessed by these servants
Know that it's God they actually did meet.

A Christmas Gift Guide

Have you made out your Christmas list yet?
Not of what to buy, but what you're hoping to get
I find most of the things that I'm sorely lacking
Wouldn't fit in the largest of Christmas stockings

I need the strength of the small sturdy beast
Who carried his burden many miles to the east
I could use some of the kindness of
the innkeeper that night
To find solutions to problems, when
there were none in sight

The persistence and faith of the traveling wise men
Who followed a star, to who knew, where or when
And since few journeys begin with an ideal start
I want some of the courage from Mary's heart

I need a little humbleness from the keepers of sheep
To believe every promise is one He will keep
And I certainly could benefit from some of the joy
Of the angels who sang the news of the newborn boy

If we could all find these gifts beneath our tree
What a wonderful place the world would be!

You've Been Called Home

Your soul is soaring, your spirit is dancing
No longer are you burdened and earth bound
And you have forever the promised peace
That only in the arms of Jesus is found

We will miss you here among us
Our sorrow is deep but our separation brief
Soon we will be together again
And eternal joy will replace the grief.

Savor the rewards of Heaven
They have been given you with Love and Grace
Your life has always glorified the Lord
Now you get to meet Him face to face

Games

If I stand on my scale in just the right place
The dial edges down, not much, just a trace
But it's enough to encourage me day after day
So even knowing it's ridiculous, I play anyway

Why do we play these little mind games?
They are rationalizations, disguised in many other names
We know they aren't real, we even know what we're doing
And yet we continue as though it's
someone else we are fooling

My conscience tells me the dishes should be done
But then again, should that really be priority number one?
There are millions of these little games that we play
The rules are simple, to get our own way

The games become dangerous however,
When they're related to sin, they are no longer clever
We rationalize our spirits warnings away
And continue to do as we want to have our own way

God tells us we must control our desires
Take responsibility for believing our own lies
When tempted beyond your strength in any way
Don't give up, fight and pray

You know what's right in your own heart
And prayer is the perfect place to start
Don't blame it on a game or name it otherwise
Keep your eyes on Jesus and your heavenly prize.

Are You Good Enough?

For years, I was the Sunday school teacher,
At every Sunday sermon, I was in my place
I daily read my bible and devotions
But ....I had never really searched for or sought God's face

I volunteered for everything
Helped clean up & took out the trash
Was kind to all, never hated anyone
Gave to the homeless, even when I was short of cash

So of course I was going to heaven
Look how very good I had been
But God said "sorry, you missed the one and only way"
"It was *my* goodness, not yours, you should have seen."

God's Voice

Once you are sure you have heard God's voice,
In answering, you really have but one choice
If you think the chicken pox were hard not to scratch
And that summer cold, you can just refuse to catch,
Just try to ignore what He wants you to do
You really won't rest, until He's heard from you

Tell Him you're busy and just can't go
That you don't have the brains to learn
the things you must know
That someone else would be a better choice
That you're not good with words and have a small voice
Tell Him you're weak, just not up to par
He created you, He knows exactly how weak you are

Of course you're not required to have strength or skill
God always provides these when you're doing His will
You will need some courage and a great deal of trust
Leave the rest of the arrangements for Him to adjust
So no excuses about how you will "see if you're free"
The only answer is: I'm ready, yes Lord, send me.

Christmas Thoughts

You think the wise men of old
Had problems finding the Christ child?
They had distance and cranky camels
But compared to our world, their distractions were mild.

We hear songs about sleigh bells, reindeer and Santa
But it's getting harder to hear about the birth of the King
Money, shopping and food take center stage
If you're not alert you could miss the
reason for the whole thing.

Parties are thrown and trees are decorated,
All just shadows of the real reason
So travel to Bethlehem within a quiet heart
And really celebrate this Christmas season.

Let's learn to look through the lights
To the perfect love they illuminate
An eternity in heaven spent with God
Is the real Christmas we should celebrate.

Is There A Hole In Your Soul?

There's not a single one of us
That isn't born with a hole in our soul
It's the space reserved to fill with God
Who we must seek and come to know

But as children we want to…"do it ourself"
And rebel against obedience and rules
And we fill that hollow with rotten stuff
To confirm that, without God, we will all act like fools.

The world offers lots of pain dulling distractions
Substances that alter the mind
People stubbornly trying to fill up their space
Without the one thing that works and is so easy to find.

It's the love of God, and it's there for the taking
A gift that He longs to give
A love and a purpose that will fill that hole
With joy and His fellowship everyday that we live.

God seeks you every day
But maybe you've never heard
How just by asking, He will clean out your junk
And fill you with His Son, His Love & His Word.

The Guest Room

When God sent me His Holy Spirit
I didn't give much thought where He would stay
I guess I figured that when He moved in
He would create a space in some magical way

Did I even worry if His room was cleaned up?
Or how big a room He was given?
Was it a peaceful spot or filled with conflict?
Was the décor too worldly or more in line with Heaven?

Did He have what He needed to do His work?
What kind of junk was I leaving in His way?
Was nourishment befitting God's Holy Spirit,
Being delivered from me each and every day?

When God's spirit comes to transform you,
What kind of accommodations will He find?
He deserves a clean, peaceful luxury suite
Prepared in Love with His purposes in mind.

How "Holey" Are You?

Each time we let temptation win
And fall,all too gleefully, into sin
We need to realize, it takes it's toll
And creates a tiny hole in our soul..

After years of accepting this is how to live
Our poor souls can hold nothing, they resemble a sieve
The word of God, His love and care
Are the only things that should be in there

Obedience is a small price to pay
To know God's heart and do things His way
God can restore your mind and your soul
To give you a life where you're completely whole.

You Believe

You believe the sun will come up tomorrow
Why so hard to believe in the one who makes it rise?
You have faith that good things will happen to you
Why are God's many blessings always such a surprise?

You see His majesty in all creation
Yet you doubt his power and might
You've been promised the Holy Spirit
And yet are discouraged you can't do right.

Acknowledge your weakness & your doubt
Ask your Lord for strength and aid
Keep your focus on the things of heaven
And claim all the loving promises He has made.

Bread From A Garbage Can

If a man gets hungry enough
He will eat bread from a garbage can
A starving traveler will go looking for spiritual food
If he finds no encouragement from his fellow man

Pray for our church, that her welcoming sanctuary
Will not become empty of bread
That the travelers we welcome will not go away hungry
And eat with the enemy from the garbage can instead

Pray for blessing and inspiration for your pastor
That each week his message fills us all
That no one goes away hungry and empty
As only God's truth can bring us to the banquet hall

Pray for continued blessing for God's church
That God's guidance and indwelling will remain
That as the body of Christ we live deserving of His favor
And fill all who come to hear the Word,
for God's honor and gain.

Wrestling Or Resting

Once again my life has changed
And God has placed me someplace scary
I can either rest in it or wrestle with it
Depending on my level of trust or my
current degree of contrary

I know that rest will bring me peace
And wrestling with God will just wear me out
But, sometimes I just can't help trying
To bring my unbelievable expertise to a
situation I know nothing about

I need to climb out of the worldly vortex
And rely on the heavenly view
Just talk to Him and humble myself
Believing He makes every situation exciting and new

He already knows my heart
I need to strive to know His and His will
Remembering always that He loves me
And ask His help to cease my striving and be still.

How He Loves Us!

Broken

Father, help me to remember
That you do *not* count it as lack of faith
When I feel broken, burdened or downcast
Instead you hold me tenderly, sharing
every tear that wets my face

I live in a world of beauty and joy
But that also has had its share of pain
And even though I trust, I don't always understand
When loss so heavily outweighs the gain

So when my heart is broken
From worldly trials and cares
Remind me Father, you have promised
That all my sorrows you will share

I look forward to the day
These troubles all will end
Until then I will believe your promises
And thank you for being there and calling me friend.

One of Your Sheep

Dear Lord Jesus
Thank you for calling me to be one of your sheep
Thank you for the promise of love, I know you will keep
Remind me each day of my need for you
And that my stubbornness precedes
most of the trouble I get into

Thinking I know where the best grass grows
I miss the sweet blessings right under my nose
In times of fear, I blindly follow the lost in front of me,
What does he know? He is just a sheep like me

Help me to faithfully listen for your voice
Knowing your guidance will provide the best choice
I'll love you dear shepherd for all of my days
And trust in your care, 'til in heaven, I peacefully graze.

Colors

When you stop and think about color
You realize it has vast, mysterious powers
Not one shade appears exactly the same,
In an entire field of blooming flowers.

Color can create emotion,
Yet our preferences have no rhyme or reason
Why is your favorite color – your favorite color?
And has your favorite changed with life's seasons?

Some colors seem to have been reserved by God
His sunsets cannot be duplicated
And the subtle, gauzy colors of the rainbow
In our attempt to capture & mimic,
always end up overstated

The many colors of the ocean,
Trees and plants with no two greens akin,
Shells and stones, red tomatoes and parrots
A rainbow trout with luminous skin

He does all of this for His children's wonder and delight
He created our world as a colorful, glorious ball
It reflects His gifts and brings Him glory
And I thank God for giving me color,
one of my favorite gifts of all.

Packing for Heaven

I only need a few things to take to Heaven
Guess I'll go pack a bag right now
I know, I know…You can't take it with you
But I think I have figured out how

I won't need any of my accumulated stuff
But I will need my lifted heart
It was given to me, totally free
Luckily, of my soul, it's become a part

I won't need money, stocks or bonds
(Don't have many of those anyway)
But I'd better take some humbleness
For my first, face to face meeting day

My gift of grace is huge,
But doesn't need to be packed
My joy and peace take up no room at all,
And my salvation doesn't need to be wrapped

Guess that's just about it
Won't need that suitcase after all
Everything I need is packed tight in my soul
So I'll be ready when He calls

A Thankful Heart

A thankful heart has benefits
It's been proven in our modern day
Lowering blood pressure, reducing stress
And keeping many illness' at bay

How can we look at all that's been given us
And not be grateful to overflowing
We cannot live one minute of our day
Without a gift from God to help us in our going

Just the sun coming up and the air we breathe
Should be enough to keep us mindful of His care
Never mind the beauty of our world
And being fearfully made to enjoy all that's there

A thankful heart will provide the way
To honor His gifts and give Him the glory
It can keep all of us humble, content & happy
And grateful 'til we reach the end of our story

Your Garden

Have you been to your own garden of Gestheme?
And knelt in prayer there
Begging God to take away your pain & discomfort
Consider for a moment, what your Lord had to bear.

The Son of Man took on the heaviest load
And it was all for the benefit of others
His sacrifice paid the debt you owe
And belief in Him will redeem you
& your sisters & brothers

Would you be willing to pay that price?
To suffer the torment and shame?
Do you even acknowledge that you've a debt to pay?
And stubbornly in your sin remain

Such love the Father has for you
That He sent His Son to take your place
To suffer and die upon His cross
So you could meet God, face to face

Humble yourself before Him,
Thank Him each and every day
He was willing to suffer and die for you
Is your obedience too high a price to pay?

My Treasure

My treasure has never been found inside a chest
Was never buried at sea
Wasn't lost and didn't need to be found
It just needed clarification from me.

For awhile my treasures were my children
They were jewels I polished for the world to see
Not just on loan from heaven above
But a possession that totally belonged to me.

Then things changed and my life fell apart
Now my treasure was a man
I trusted him above all else
That also turned out to be a foolish plan

Then for awhile my treasure was food
If the pantry was full, I was rich
My treasure has also been money and pride
Counting on these, sent life into a ditch

Sending my deposits to heaven
Has been the saving, savings plan
God pays interest like no one else
Not money or food or children or man.

You never know when you're going to go
And you can't take it with you when you do
Just keep enough for your day to day needs
And let God have the rest for a miracle or two

Thank God You're A Girl

Did you ever wish you'd been born a man?
You silly, silly girl
You hold such a special place in your master's mind
Your little heart should be constantly awhirl.

So many integral parts of God's perfect plan
You were created to be and do
You are loved and equipped like no other creature
There is no other exactly like you.

You have been entrusted to carry beneath your heart
The entirety of the next generation
And endowed with special wisdom and patience
To nourish and establish this special creation

You've been given enough strength to encourage
And enough softness to comfort and heal
You can lead an army or bandage a knee
With God as your anchor and your keel

Like our Lord, you can shoulder great sorrow
But your joy can be heard 'round the world
So, let's remember to thank Him every day
For being that special blessing of the
Most High, His beloved daughter,
.....A girl

The Shadows of Christmas

The shadows of Christmas
Swirl all around the holiday
But we must look behind the shadows
To find the real meaning of Christmas day

The Christmas trees we carry home
Plain and bound tightly up with twine
Stand transformed on Christmas morning
Free and full of light that shines.

This should cause us to remember
That we too were once bound and tied
Then our Savior appeared among us
And invited us to live, as He took
our sin and willingly died.

The piles of gifts beneath the tree
Are wrapped in paper and pretty string
But until we unwrap and accept the gift
The box may as well be empty, the
salvation He offers is everything

The feasting and making merry,
The love that fills our hearts
Are the over flow of gratitude
For the eternal kingdom, of which we've been made a part

So while we treasure the shadows
The tradition and all the rest
Let's not forget *why* the baby came
And that the gift He offers, Salvation, is the very best

I Hope There's Dirt in Heaven

I've heard Heaven has streets paved in gold
City walls adorned in jewels
It all sounds so beautiful, however,
If I could make one small appeal….

I hope there's dirt in Heaven
And trees and rocks and raging rivers,
Mountains, deserts and even cactus
Sunsets with colors that give you shivers.

Pine cones and daisies and a few lady bugs
Trumpet vines and rose bushes galore
Wandering, rutted country lanes
Old barns with chickens, cows and more

I've read that the sea will disappear
And with it of course the whales,
No more dolphins or octopi
No more masted ships with great billowing sails.

Now please don't misunderstand,
I'm not saying I don't want to go
I would just love to find some dirt in Heaven
Under the golden glow.

If He Didn't Love Me

If He didn't love me,
The earth would be barren and mean
Instead of the incredible beauty
That is mine to be seen

If He didn't love me
There would be no plan
For the problem of sin
And the reconciliation of God and man

If He didn't love me
No grace would be given
To rejoin me with God
To be blessed and forgiven

If He didn't love me
No savior would have been sent
To bear my sin on his body
To die in my place, broken and spent

If He didn't love me
His son wouldn't have risen
To release me and free me
From my sin imposed prison

If He didn't love me
I would have no hope
No strength and no purpose
And no reason to cope

If He didn't love me
He wouldn't have shown me the way
To spend eternity in heaven
With the Father, Son and Spirit, some sweet day

When the Cock Crows

How the Apostle Peter must have cringed
The minute he heard that cock crow
Our Lord had told him it would happen
But faced with his denial, Bitter shame did he know.

How many times in a day
Do I hear that raucous sound?
And realize I have denied my Lord
By careless speech or not standing my ground

The cock crows only in my head,
But can you imagine the din?
If he crowed for real, right out loud
Every time we turned our backs and fell into sin?

Lord, grant me the strength to follow you
And keep that cock from crowing
When I begin to have whole days of quiet
I'll praise you for it and know that I'm growing

MARK 14:30-31

Do You Know Someone?

Do you know someone who hasn't seen the sun in years?
Who's suffered more than their share,
whole days filled with tears.
You think that surely life will soon cut them some slack,
That it's time they had a bit of a break,
got that load off their back

But even if it seems fair for things to
let up, it's not necessarily so
They may still have a bigger mountain to
climb and a much longer way to go
What can you say to those friends? You
feel guilty for having it so good.
You can share with them the hope that
endures, the hope that has long stood

Jesus has overcome the world, with all of its grief and pain
And once you are a child of His, there's
no need to go back again
Rest in his loving arms, find comfort in his plan
The trials teach us to rely on Him, no
matter their length or span.

The Heart of Sue

The heart of Sue is broken
But she's not sure she wants you to know
It's sad and scary and worrisome
There's been a major rupture in her life's flow

Of course, her entire family has left her
Some have gone to heaven, others just away
And her once strong flight feathers
Feel unable to lift her on any given day

But she has friends and she has God
So all the love she needs is there
Still, she must walk this trail alone
To arrive at healing with light & peace beyond compare

As she travels up this road
The love of God is always within reach
And through Him, the love of her friends
Will hasten this walk and put wings on her feet

Grief is a part of living
Just not the most fun part
But our strength and prayers and love provide help
And God will surely quickly mend my friend, Sue's heart

Stubborn Child

Oh Lord, When you chasten me
And I stubbornly hold to my own way
Help me to know that you still love me
And my failure to yield is what makes you feel far away.

I will question your authority,
I doubt your almighty power
And still insist on putting myself first
Even in my darkest hours.

Sometimes you leave me lost a little while
To wander on my own
To show me how much I really need you
But then you always bring me home.

Your faithfulness is amazing
Your love beyond the scope of my mortal brain
And my gratefulness for your tender care,
Will forever, a part of me remain.

A Gift

With loves perfect knowledge, the selection was easy
God knew exactly what gift was needed
The presentation would be simple
A forever gift, with benefits and hopes exceeded.

He enlisted the help of a few of His faithful
Their belief left their obedience unquestioned
To wait on God until the perfect time
The parts they played would go humbly unmentioned

When the gift was finally presented
It was enough for everyone to share
And yet was chosen for each individual
Born of a plan so great and a love so rare

I'm writing this note on Christmas, Lord
To thank you for my savior, my beautiful gift
I know I'll never need another thing
Each Christmas, for as long as I live.

Mystical Experiences

There is no lack of mystical experiences
You've been living in one since before your birth
Your human body and the way it works,
Makes you a "mystical experience" of infinite worth.

The air you breathe, the sun on your face
Life from the dirt that brings forth food
The beauty and majesty of our planet earth
All prove that God, is indeed, good.

The intricate workings of nature
Each creation with its own season
The beauty and wonder in each of these
All given for us, but not without reason

What holds all of these mysteries in place?
But God's mighty hand from heaven above
They are there to show us what's possible
If we just accept and live in His love

"Love makes the world go round"
Is more than just a saying,
Without it, all would cease to exist
It's for more love, that we should all be praying.

And love itself is a mystical experience
Without definition or explanation
Is love just chemicals?, I don't think so.
Mystery is a planned part of God's creation.

Why did that person come into my life?
Isn't it odd how that all worked out?
Was I just saved from certain disaster?
What is life really all about?

So I look for these mystical experiences every day
They make me grateful and fill me with awe
I always gain a whole new perspective on life
What a wonderful mystical gift has been given us all.

The Aftermath of Easter

Some events are so life changing
It's impossible for the old perspective to remain
And because of that very first Easter
Here are a few things, that for me, will never be the same.

Because of Easter:
When someone now abandons me
And cowardice causes them to run
I know that fear has overcome their will
And though I wanted more for them,
I needn't come undone.

Because of Easter:
I see that no suffering is ever in vain
Pain sometimes part of the larger eternal plan
He is always there to hold us together
To reconcile the holy heart of God
to the lowly heart of man.

Because of Easter:
I will never again see a stone blocking my way
That can't be moved, no matter how big it is,
Or how long or how deep I have buried myself
The promise of resurrection is a promise of His.

Because of Easter:
I will ask forgiveness for myself and others
With grace and an understanding heart
Because I know He forgave me first
So that of His kingdom, I could become a part.

Because of Easter:
Every gift I will ever receive
Can never begin to compare
To the precious gift He gave to me
Easter reminds me to handle it with care.

Because of Easter:
There is nothing that will not be proved by Love
And in it, are power and glory and might
That God so loved the world, He gave it His son
To teach us and heal us, that we may
become perfect in His sight.

When I'm Gone

For all the days my love surrounded you
Even when I was out of sight
Please remember that it's still around you
Even though my soul has taken flight

I will still watch over you
And I'll still care that you wisely choose
That you're kind to yourself and others
And respectful of the earth's gifts you use

I hope you realize that God loves you
Way beyond your knowing
And there's always a harvest of some kind
For every seed you've been sowing

Love is the only thing you have
That will truly last forever
All else will end in God's perfect timing
Then once again we will be together

Don't Look Back

So, your life didn't turn out exactly as planned
Well, few lives seldom do
Decisions are hard and life is messy
We all foul it up, somehow, on our way through

But living in a past full of regret
Is not a good place to stay
Keep moving forward, there's hope in the future
And, don't look back, you're not going that way

Little Lamb

Little lamb, you crave comfort every day
And ignore the shepherds voice you hear
Thinking you are wise and strong
You hide and pretend that He's not all that near

The shepherd knows the snow is coming
And you would be better off down the hill
But you don't want to move or walk all that way
You bravely ignore the clouds and the chill

Sometimes, the shepherd must pick you up
And carry you to where you belong
And you still don't see the reason for it all
You're fine on your own, wise and strong

You may never see the danger the storm will bring
Because the shepherd has brought you safely home
If only you knew how much He loves you
When He calls, you would quickly and willingly come

You would think by now you would trust Him
And follow wherever He leads
He's protected you from wolves & danger
And even saves you from your own misdeeds

Your shepherd was called to give His life
To save the wandering and the lost
And yet His spirit still loves you and leads you
For your salvation, He paid the cost.

Don't Look, God

Has this ever been you?
Sadly, it has several times been me
When I found myself doing things
I didn't want God to see.

I wished that I could ask Him
To please turn around or close his eyes
When I was gossiping or in a rage
Behaving <u>not</u> like a child of His, being totally unwise.

I wanted to be sure He <u>was</u> watching
When I gave to that homeless man
Or taught that Sunday school class
Or purposely surrendered to His plan

Of course I know He sees me all the time
Looks right into my heart
And what I can't finish right in front of God
I know I shouldn't even start.

The Three Legged Race

I asked the Lord for the thousandth time
To grant me awareness of His presence
I wanted to feel the "walking together"
In more than just an intellectual sense

I constantly found myself "back in the world"
Having let the awareness of Him slip away
I needed to find a way to hold Him close
Throughout each minute of every day.

Faithful at always, God spoke to my heart
And wiped the tears from my face
He said," If it will help you, child,
Think of your life as a three legged race".

When two have only three legs to walk on
One cannot move forward without the other
The minute one tries to go his own way
He will stumble and fall and need help to recover.

If you will submit yourself to this mode of travel
And rely on Jesus to lead the way
He will walk beside you, providing the balance
His arm close around you, throughout every day.

The Unexpected

The unexpected is just one of the tools
The good Lord uses to keep us aware
Of His sovereignty and control of our universe
But also of his love and care

If things always unfolded
Just as we imagined in our little minds
Who would seem always in control then?
We already think the best thing He created is mankind

So God throws a few curveballs
While we're standing at the plate
Just to help us realize, we're not in charge
And at running things, we're really, just not all that great.

A Request of the King

Is it because your mountain is so high
That I often fail to reach you?
Let me hold on to your deep love for me
And know that you will always see me through

Help me to surrender each distraction
And take captive every errant thought
To learn that irritation, anger and impatience
Are useless feelings, not from you, and all for naught

Let any pride found in me
Be only from knowing you
Let all my strength be spent in service
Any movement only after acknowledging you

Let my joy be found in bringing you honor
And let me covet no glory for my own
Let me serve and love you always
And seat you justly on my heart's throne

Let me never fail to praise you
Keep me mindful of all you are
I treasure the awareness of your presence
And thank you for walking with me this far.

Silly Head

Ever since creation, God has been trying to teach us
His character, His plans, His ways
But, being the blind, sinful humans we are
We don't want to listen and find it hard to obey

His word tells us of Christ's coming
And even explains, what He's coming for
Over 400 times His word contains the good news
He showed us miracles and healings
and we still demanded more

God has sent prophets, angels, and even His son
To help us to understand
But yet today some are still stumbling and questioning
Distracted by the world and the folly of man.

It's time we studied God's word, like
our lives depend upon it
Because they do, just as He has always said
So before it's too late, heed the words of a very wise child,
"Just believe what God says, silly head"

The Church Elephant

There is an elephant that's started attending our church
He sits in the very front row,
Lots of people realize he's there
But won't let anyone else know that they know

Friends have left the congregation
But the why is still unaddressed
What rules were broken, whose feelings were hurt,
Was it God or the church that was going unblessed?

Most folks seem to think, if untalked about
The elephant just might go away
Or when the gossip finally dies down
He will leave and go merrily on his way

Hopefully we won't get too comfortable
And decide that he should stay
His presence is NOT encouraging
For new believers brought our way

We must search our hearts and our bibles
To see what God thinks we should do
And restore our church to the center of His will
And pledge ourselves to His purposes anew.

What I'm Thankful For

How can I number the things I'm grateful for?
We'd be here for a year and a day
My list is so long it would wrap the earth twice
And even then, there would be more to say.

I'm so thankful God kept pursuing me
Long after the Garden of Eden fall
That He didn't just turn His back and walk away
And rue the day, he created us at all.

And when we continued in stubborn sin
He loved me enough to plan for a way
I could be with Him forever and ever
But what a price His only Son had to pay.

There's a lot of other things, I daily enjoy
That have been given to me free of charge
But they are nothing without my salvation
Nothing I'm thankful for looms quite as large.

About the Author

Karen has been rhyming most of her adult life and has used rhyme for everything from advice to her children and grandchildren to marketing promotions for companies such as Union Bank of California, Goodwill Industries and Century 21 Real Estate. This collection of Christian poetry is her simple testimony to the joy of having God in her life.

Printed in the United States
By Bookmasters